CW01373353

I wanted this to last.

Nathalie Saldana

Copyright © 2012 Author Name

All rights reserved.

ISBN:
9798392238965

dedication

This book is dedicated to my first love.
maybe we were too young,
or maybe we just weren't meant to be.
either way,
I will never forget you and the lessons you taught me.

Table of Contents

Chapters

love	1
denial	46
anger	78
bargaining	112
depression	139
acceptance	186

I have created a playlist of songs that have
helped inspire each emotion into words,
I recommend giving it a listen while you read.

Or try typing
I wanted this to last
Nathalie kristine on Spotify!

I wanted this to last

my first love

love

love

It was almost two years ago,
but I still remember this one conversation we had.
You told me you would write a book about our love,
so that we could give it to our children,
a way to make sure our love would never be forgotten,
even long after we were.

I looked at you and smiled.
Maybe one day you'll write our book.

// I still hope my kids know about our love story.
-nathalie kristine

I wanted this to last

The moment I first saw you
still vivid in my mind,
you sat lonely in the corner with your knees side by side,
you looked a little too drunk
I could tell by your glossy eyes of crystal blue.
I don't know what it was
but something was drawing me to you.

I think it was the person that was hidden
behind your gorgeous blue eyes,
I can tell you have the sweetest soul inside.

I knew nothing about you,
but for some reason,
you still felt so familiar.

// maybe we have met in another life.
-nathalie kristine

love

In my hand was the first note you gave me,
to this day it's still one of my favorite memories.

"I want this to last"
that is all it said,
a tear escaped my eye
as your words echoed In my head.

I want this to last too,

I wanted this to last

> I want this
> to last
> ♡
>
> WE'RE NOT REALLY STRANGERS

// I'll cherish your note forever.
-nathalie kristine

love

I was sitting on the couch
when I felt a hand patting my head,
you looked down at me & smiled.
How silly,
that a pat brought me so much joy.
I looked back at you and laughed.
Even in a crowded room you were always close to me.

It was those smallest of moments,
that stained my memory

// a simple moment, but a cherished memory.
-nathalie kristine

I wanted this to last

When I gaze into your eyes,
I see the parts of you that you try to hide,
all the broken parts that you learned to suppress,
you internalize all of your own distress.

but I notice those hidden parts of you,
as if you're someone I always knew.

like a familiar feeling I once felt,
Those parts of you,
remind me of myself.

// If only I could tell you i hide all those parts of me too
-nathalie kristine

love

I want to love you in all the ways
I've longed to be loved.

// You deserve to know what it's like to be loved.

-nathalie kristine

Your arms are my safe-haven.

When the future weighs heavy on my mind,
you are there to wrap yourself around me.

When I can't help but cry about the past,
your hands are there to wipe away every tear.

In moments of life's presents mess,
my favorite place is a spot on your chest.

> *// you are my escape*
> *-nathalie kristine*

love

I see so much potential in you
I pray one day you'll see it too.

Promise me, you won't give up?
Although you may be unaware of your potential,
it does exist,
far beyond what you tell yourself.
I will not stop pushing you forward
until you can see,
how wonderful your future is supposed to be.

// don't hold yourself to the past.
- nathalie kristine

I wanted this to last

I will never forget that one summer night,
we were both so young, and naive.
You had a bit too much to drink,
and I promised I'd drive you home.

Those three words slipped from your mouth
as you closed my car door,
" goodnight, I love you. "
You probably didn't hear me
but I whispered back
"I love you too."

// it was that night I realized I was in love with you.
-nathalie kristine

love

I started writing to you every night,
I have a journal that I keep secret.

between the pages are the memories of our days
each entry filled, with the little details.
I write in it every night before I go to sleep.
I want us to always remember the years we spend together,
every detail, without any memory being lost to time.

// I plan to give it to you on our wedding day.
-nathalie kristine

I wanted this to last

There is a perfect spot on your chest
where I lay my head and rest,
to the sound of your heart beating.

In your loving embrace,
I have found my safe place.

If only these moments weren't so fleeting.

// oh how I love to listen to your heart beating.
　　-nathalie kristine

love

my fingers are intertwined with yours,
just as our souls have become.

> *// our souls interlinked.*
> *-nathalie kristine*

You have become my home.

When you embrace me
my head falls right into your heart,
I can hear it beating as you pull me closer.
I feel a sense of belonging,
as if I just found home.

I wish you would never let me go,
nothing can describe the warmth of feeling at home.

// your arms are a house I don't want to leave.
-nathalie kristine

love

I think one of the deepest expressions of love
someone could ever give is praying to their God about you.

All religions aside,
imagine someone who loves you so much,
that they talk to God about you.
The God that created the universe,
and that has power over everything.
The God that carved every mountain into place,
and could give you anything if you just asked,
and yet,
They choose to pray about you.
You might never fully understand but I chose
to pray about you every single night.

I would ask God to stand by your bedside,
and watch over you as you sleep.
I would pray for him to heal your heart of all
the pain you can't seem to speak about.
I would pray for him to grant you his peace,
and for him to never leave your side.

I prayed for your healing,
before I ever prayed for mine.

// and I have never stopped praying about you.
-nathalie kristine

I wanted this to last

I have never wrote about anyone,
In the ways I write about you.

// and I never will.
-nathalie kristine

love

How do you make the most mundane things,
feel as if it's the most exciting experience?

Basic every day tasks feel like I'm a child doing
something for the very first time.
Every night we cook dinner together and we slow dance
 in my kitchen, You'll twirl me around as we laugh,
and we forget all about dinner we have cooking.

 // life used to be boring, but never with you.
-nathalie kristine

I wanted this to last

On the nights when I can't sleep
I admire you as you lay next to me.
I listen to your heart beating as it
 matches up with my breathing.

You pull me closer to you,
and I whisper to God,
to tell him all about you.

if only you knew,
how often I whisper to God,
just to talk about you.

// I think I made God fall in love with you too.
-nathalie kristine

love

I fell in love with your family,
as silly as that sounds.

Your mother has the same deep blue eyes as you,
your sister's laugh always reminded me of yours,
and your brother has the same love of nature that you do.
I found pieces of you in each of your family members.

In one way or another,
they reminded me of all the reasons
I fell in love with you.

// they all carry pieces of you.
*   -nathalie kristine*

I wanted this to last

I hope one day you will understand
the depth of the love I have for you.

// if only you knew how much I think about you.
-nathalie kristine

love

You have helped heal me by showing me
what love is in the simplest of ways.

I told you once how much I love the wild flowers we
sometimes pass along the road, now every time we are driving
I noticed you watch for patches of them.
You stop the car and smile brightly at me,
I watch as you run out and pick me the prettiest bouquet.
I promise I'll keep every flower that I get.

Whenever we are talking on the phone you make sure
we never hang up without saying I love you,
It doesn't matter if we are fighting,
or if you are angry,
You will tell me in your grumpy tone of voice
"Goodbye....
I love you."
if for some reason I forget to say it,
you'll call me right back until I do.

Every night we spend together you cook me dinner,
and you make sure I finish all my food.

You take care of me,
in the ways I've struggled to take care of myself.

That is love.

// you have shown me a love I have never known.
- nathalie kristine

I wanted this to last

Sometimes I think about those summer nights,
we'd stay up so late just talking inside my car.
I'd drive you home and park right outside your house.

I didn't want you to go inside,
you didn't wanna go either.

You'd look me in the eyes and almost say goodbye,
But then you pull me in to kiss you,
and come up with any excuse for you not to go inside.

// we were so young and so in love.
  -nathalie kristine

love

You are my first love,
I pray you will also be my last.

Nobody has ever made me safe like you do.
I've never been given reasons to trust the hands,
I placed my heart in.
My walls have always been up,
and my alarms always on.
I have only ever loved in a constant
state of fight or flight.

That was until I met you.

// my heart finally feels safe with you.
-nathalie kristine

I wanted this to last

You took me to your secret spot,
somewhere in the mountains surrounded by trees,
a place you've only ever shown to me.
We explored the mountains together
until we stumbled across a perfect tree.

You carved your name, and then helped me carve mine.
Our names are right next to each other,
 in the only spot left unmarked,
proof of our love is now etched in the bark.

And if time goes by and we both grow apart,
at least our names will remain with carved into that tree,
holding together a precious memory.

// I wonder if we will ever go back to that tree.
-nathalie kristine

love

Being with you feels so safe,
you make me feel loved in ways
I have never been shown before.

I enjoy being in calm love.
It feels like warm blanket wrapped around
my tattered heart.

// your love makes me feel at peace.
*　-nathalie kristine*

I wanted this to last

You calm my mind, my body, my soul
you put my pieces together to make me feel whole.

// my negative emotions subside when I'm with you.
-nathalie kristine

love

You always talk about how much you can't wait to marry me,
My future feels so safe with you.

You notice whenever I see rings that I like.
We were at the yearly carnival when I pointed one out to you.

" look at how beautiful this one sparkles
and how gorgeous the heart shape is"

You turn to me and with the biggest
 smile you pick it up,
" I'll buy it for you."

I giggle with happiness as you hand the merchant cash,
You pretend to propose to me with it
and put it on my ring finger.
It feels as if it's always belonged there.

"it's my promise"
you whisper to me as I watch it sparkle
 from all the carnival lights.

// I never will lose that silly carnival ring.
   -nathalie kristine

I wanted this to last

I once asked God what love was supposed to be like,
that's when you walked into my life.

// your presence brings me a familiar peace.
-nathalie kristine

love

There was just something about being so young,
and falling so deeply in love.
It felt as if nothing else in the world mattered,
we could do anything as long as we had each other.

No matter what tragedies could lie in our path,
As long as I have you,
I know it will come to pass.

// I still feel like I'm 19 and in love with you.
-nathalie kristine

I wanted this to last

The beauty I see in you is so much deeper than
the bright blue of your eyes, or perfectly placed freckles
on both of your cheeks;

I see the tenderness in your heart,
I hear the softness in your voice,
I feel the gentleness in your touch.

What made me fall in love was
all the parts of you think go ignored

*// but I noticed everything people have
overlooked about you.
-nathalie kristine*

love

There is one thing that I will promise you,
Just as I love your beauty,
I will love your ugly too.

The overwhelming anger you can't seem to control,
caused from all your sadness that has never been consoled.

The emotionless front you put on for everyone,
we both know it won't last in the long run.
You play it so well you almost convince yourself too,
but deep down your emotions seep through.
Your heavy denial of your own faults and all the lies you tell
me when you fear the consequences of the truth.
I promise I will still love all those parts of you too.

There's is no such thing as a person without flaws,
But love doesn't care,
It does not stop because of our faults.

So as I fall in love with the beautiful parts of you,
I promise I will continue to love the ugly parts too.

// do you promise to love the flawed parts of me too?
   -nathalie kristine

I wanted this to last

I never wore my seatbelt,
I just didn't have a care.

But when I get into my car with you,
you make sure I have my seatbelt on,
you won't drive away until I do.

It is in the smallest things you do,
when I hear the loudest

" I love you. "

// you care about me in ways I haven't cared for myself.
-nathalie kristine

love

You brought back parts of myself
I thought had been forever lost.
My hope that a love for me exists,
and the possibility that someone could understand me.
You repaired my heart,
and bandaged up my wounds,
you showed me love without misuse.

The calmness of love.

// I never knew that calm love existed
-nathalie kristine

I wanted this to last

I'll forever cherish the nights when
we danced in my kitchen.

// I hate dancing, but I will always dance with you.
　-nathalie kristine

love

You are peacefully asleep in my lap,
while I try to count all of your freckles.
I whisper to you quietly so I don't disturb your sleep,
and I tell you how much you really mean to me.

I listen to your breathing as it matches up with mine.
It is in those precious moments,
when there's is no such thing as time.

// one day I will count every freckle on your cheeks.
-nathalie kristine

I wanted this to last

If only you knew what I think about you.

I wish I could describe the peace I feel,
just laying next to you.
I wish you knew how I describe you to strangers,
and all the things that remind me of you.
Or how I imagine that our hearts are holding hands,
every time you are holding mine.

If only you knew what it's like
to be in love with you.

// there's so many things I wish you knew.
-nathalie kristine

love

Sex is something that I hold so dearly.
It is those parts of me that are the most precious,
I was not meant for just anyone to experience.

I want my body to be cherished, to be loved.
I don't want to be used for pleasure by a
man who will only lust after me.

Real love is resisting the temporary desire
 of a short-lasting pleasure.
An act of self-control,
 to prove the knowledge of the difference
 between both love and lust.
Lust is a short-lived burning fire,
while love is something that can never be put out.
 I know a man will never truly cherish me,
if he can't even wait for me.

Today I told you we couldn't have sex anymore,
you told me that wasn't the part of me you fell for.

// I've never met a man like you before.
-nathalie kristine

I wanted this to last

There are deep levels of intimacy,
loving someone without having sex with them.
When I get too drunk and we're alone in bed
you could easily take advantage of me,
but instead,
you protect every boundary I have set.

A love without lust.

// that is the purest love I have ever known.
  -nathalie kristine

love

July is my favorite month we've spent together,
with late summer nights,
and visits to the flower-filled canyons.

We've done so many things that I've always wanted to do;
like when we went in that hot air balloon,
or going to the lantern festival,
and that trip we took with your family to the beach
or when we traveled outside the country.

July has been filled with so many summer sunsets,
when we lay close to each other cuddling under the blankets.
We watch as the sky fades from a bright orange to dark blue.

I'll never forget the month of July because of you.

// I kept the journal is full of our memories.
-nathalie kristine

I wanted this to last

I keep every flower you give me, even to this day.
I've hung them all up on my bedroom walls,
each flower has its own display.

My favorite ones are the handpicked flowers,
I stare at them hung up on my wall,
It feels as if it was yesterday.

you would stop the car,
run out with a big smile on your face,
and return with the most beautiful bouquet.

I keep every petal that falls off them compiled,
because those are the petals that will be used
when I walk down the aisle.
And as time goes on,
you will still pick me flowers that I will save,
and I hope to be buried with them in my grave.

// I promise I'll keep every flower you give me.
-nathalie kristine

I love you enough to understand you.
I don't know why you can't love me,
like how I love you.

I love you enough to attempt to see your
reasoning in everything,
I got to know all the hidden corners in your mind,
But have you gotten to know mine?

I just wish you'd want to know me,
as deeply as I've gotten to know you.

I feel an ache to be understood,
but I'm afraid
nobody ever could.

// why haven't you gotten to know me?
*   -nathalie kristine*

I wanted this to last

What if my mind is just too much
 for anyone to ever understand?

I have spent so much time
trying to figure out everyone else,
yet I don't even know myself.

How could I ever expect you to see all of my mental agony,
when I have chosen to suffer silently.

Can I actually blame you,
If you never even knew?

// is it my fault for never telling you about the pain I was in?
  -nathalie kristine

love

The loneliness of not being understood,
what a desolate feeling.
I would be laying next to you,
but it was as if we were in different worlds.

You never even tried to understand me
the way I understand you.

// but I don't want to leave you.
    -nathalie kristine

I wanted this to last

I wanted this to last

denial

denial

I don't want to give up on us,
I don't want it to be over.
I keep thinking of everything I never got to tell you,
and all of the plans we never got to live through;
The goals we made together,
that house we were supposed to build,
the baby names we picked out,
our scrapbook that never got to be filled.

So tell me is there something I can do?
Or anything I could say to you?
Something to quickly change your mind,
before we lose each other in the vicious hands of time.

Please just tell me before it becomes too late,
I don't want the end of us to be our fate.

// is it already too late?
 -nathalie kristine

I wanted this to last

Please will you linger behind my door
a few seconds longer,
just to make sure.

Please come back inside,
just listen.
Is losing your first love the right decision?

// I guess self sabotage is my addiction.
    -nathalie kristine

denial

I lay in bed all alone,
no one coming home to ask me if
I have eaten anything today.

The numbness that hunger brings helps drown
out the pain of your absence.

I haven't eaten in days.

// the gnawing pain of emptiness in my stomach,
is better than the constant pit of despair.
*   -nathalie kristine*

I wanted this to last

I can never start over with someone new,
I will always be haunted by the ghost of you.

// are you haunted by the memories of we used to be?
-nathalie kristine

denial

I've convinced myself that you will show up at my door
carrying a bouquet of yellow flowers,
just like how you used to always do.

I can't wait to jump into your arms and hug you again,
I've spent the last weeks reflecting on where I went wrong,
and I found solutions to all of our old issues.

I hope you've been doing the same.
I can't wait to tell you about it all,
I will be waiting by my door.

I don't know if you're coming,
a month has now passed,
and my messages get no reply.

You promised you wouldn't leave
without saying goodbye.

Maybe you're just busy.
I'll keep waiting by the door for you.

// every time I hear a knock I hope it's you.
-nathalie kristine

I wanted this to last

I can still remember the feeling you left me with
the night we told each other goodbye.
I gave you one last hug before we both walked away,
I tried so hard to memorize your scent before it faded.

My arms wrapped tightly around your neck,
as I pulled your body close to me.
 my head rested against your chest,
and I could hear your precious heart beating,
for the very last time.
your arms never embraced me back,
you just stood there staring at me with empty eyes,
while I was trying to memorize every last part of you.

did I ever mean anything to you?
I could tell by the emptiness in your eyes,
you have already forgotten me.

// I wish you wanted to remember me.
   - nathalie kristine

denial

I've always hated cigarettes.

Growing up I watched as they'd take over the lives of
people who were closest to me.
I still remember being 7 years old and smelling
the cigarette scent for the very first time.
I was with my childhood best friend,
back when we would always play pretend with
the barbies in her grandparent's living room.
The smoke would fill up the room as they watched us play,
I would begin to feel suffocated,
and the smell would overwhelm my undeveloped lungs.
I tried to continue to play,
but that horrible smell didn't go away.

I remember being only 16 watching my first boyfriend smoke
so many cigarettes until he couldn't breathe anymore.
He'd cough until his face turned purple,
and then reach for another one in his pack.
I hated the taste of it on his lips.
Sometimes he'd only smoke them just to spite me,
and blow the cigarette smoke in my face.
He enjoyed seeing me suffer to breathe.
It was his addiction that caused me to leave.

I remember being 18 and meeting you by chance,
you were holding a wretched cigarette in your hand.
I told myself not to fall in love, but I thought I could fix you.
I wanted to help save you from the hands of addiction.
but instead,
I watched as they slowly ruined you.

Every morning I would wake up to the sound of
your coughing lungs aching to be set free.
Your own body is screaming at you,
Yet its cries for help were drowned out by another cigarette.

I wanted this to last

I expressed my concern about your health, and you told me
you wanted to free yourself.
I did everything I could to help you cut ties with addiction,
But in the end, it was all your decision.

For a short time,
the taste of cigarettes was not on your tongue,
you no longer had to spit up all the mucus
built up inside your lungs.
The life returned to your face,
I watched as you became free of your addiction.
I was so proud of you.
It was all your decision.

Months have passed,
and we are no longer together.
I can still vividly recall how I felt when I learned
 you returned to your cigarette addiction.
all the progress you made,
how could you just throw it all away?
The lungs you had once set free,
only to go back to the same exact suffering.

denial

I can still remember when I questioned it all,
I was drunk & missing you,
and the closest thing I could get to being on your lips
was smoking a cigarette.
I watched myself fall victim to the very thing
I watched ruin you.

The smoke left my lungs and took over my throat,
and I began to smell that same familiar scent,
the one I have always hated.
Only this time, it was comforting.
What began as "just one" cigarette to remind me
what it felt like to be around you
is now something I reach for every time I miss you.

I have always hated cigarettes.

*// The scent I used to hate so much
became the one I found comfort in.
-nathalie kristine*

I wanted this to last

I don't know if I'll ever be able to accept
how things between us ended.
I fear acceptance.
If I accept that you are no longer mine,
and I am no longer yours,
I will start to forget everything about you;
our memories will slowly become replaced,
and all the days we spent together will fade away.

I fear that I will not be able to recall
what it felt like every time I'd kiss you,
or how your voice sounded every night
when you'd pull me close and whisper
 " I love you."

I dread the day when my memory of you
no longer lingers.

// you will be buried somewhere deep in the back of my mind
   -nathalie kristine

denial

My family has been asking about you,
they want to know what happened between us,
and why you haven't showed up.
I don't know the answer.

How did this mess of us come to be?
We used to always brag about how
loving each other came so easily.

I told them that nothing has happened,
and you'll soon be knocking on our door,
but deep down the truth is,
I'm not really sure.

// I'm not sure if you'll ever come back.
  -nathalie kristine

I wanted this to last

I'd rather wallow in our memories forever
than forget the love we once had.

// maybe one day I will be able to relive those moments.
  - nathalie kristine

denial

I've been saving you a seat at church for weeks now.
Whenever someone asks if it's taken
I tell them you're just running late.

The emptiness of the chair next to me
drowns out the sounds of prayer.
All I can think about is your promise.
Why didn't you keep your promise?
You told me you would be here,
at least once.

I stopped going to church.
Not because I lost faith in God,
but because I lost faith in you.

The empty chair beside me would haunt me as I tried to pray.
You're the only thing I can pray about now.

// I kept thinking you'd be there one day.
   -nathalie kristine

I wanted this to last

I keep making excuses for you,
I tell myself that you didn't mean to hurt me,
and all the lies you told me was only to protect me.
I tell myself that you're still a good person,
you just don't understand your own emotions.
I remind myself that hurt people,
hurt people, and hurting me meant that
you were hurting too.
I keep making excuses for you so that
I can continue to love you without feeling
as if I am betraying myself.

But the truth is no matter how many excuses I make for you,
you have chose to hurt me,
Continuously.
You held me in your arms as I sobbed,
you comforted the pain that you caused,
and yet still you did it again,
and again,
and again.

you were once a good person to me,
but you are no longer good to me anymore.

// sometimes I convince myself you're still the sweet boy I once knew.
-nathalie kristine

denial

I know we are both hurt, but tell me,
how you are okay leaving me with no answer?
I don't understand.

Am I not worthy of a simple explanation?
I know you don't love me anymore,
So why do you keep telling me you do?
I know the truth already,
just fucking say it to me.

// I don't want to hold onto the lies you tell me.
        -nathalie kristine

I wanted this to last

Can we just pretend, just for one night?
that nothing happened,
that nothing changed.
You can come over while I am sleeping and kiss me awake,
I'll jump right into your arms and beg you to cuddle with me,
but instead you'll tickle me and I'll hold back my laugh.

I'll make you a cup of tea while you cook us dinner,
and we'll kiss every chance we get,
as we dance in my kitchen.
I'll ask you about your day while you set our plates,
you'll answer me and complain how much your body aches.

Afterward, I'll grab your hand and drag you with me
we'll brush our teeth and get ready for bed.
I'll cuddle up into my favorite spot on your chest,
as you plant a kiss right on my forehead.
We can listen to bible stories for one last time,
right before we fall asleep.

Just for one night, everything will feel okay..
I won't remember how you left me,
you won't remember how I hurt you.

For more one night we can just pretend it's July again.

// can we just go back to July?
-nathalie kristine

denial

Sometimes I get so drunk that I forget you're not
the same person who loved me anymore.

I start to smile at the thought of you,
and my mind drifts back to the night
when we first said I love you,
We were both so young,
we had so much hope for the future
we were determined to build.

It's nice not to remember who you are now.
but It doesn't last long before I realize,
it's not the past anymore,
and we are both not who we once were.

// do you ever remember who I used to be?
   -nathalie kristine

I wanted this to last

I wish the absence of you
didn't feel like the absence of myself.

// you have pieces of me that no longer exist.
*   -nathalie kristine*

denial

If I leave you alone for long enough
will you come back?
I know my love can be suffocating at times,
It's never on purpose.

Sometimes I wish I could have distance from myself too.

// I'm sorry I'm so hard to love.
  -nathalie kristine

I wanted this to last

I still talk about you as if we are still together,
I don't want to face the truth that you're gone.

// I catch myself talking about you as if we're still together.
　　　　-nathalie kristine

denial

What about everything we planned?
Like that trip we were supposed to take,
or what about all the Christmases you'll miss?
What happened to experiencing this life together,
and everything we were supposed to accomplish?

I was going to teach you how to scrapbook,
and you were gonna teach me how to fish.
We had so many plans,
how did you just give up so easily?
I just don't understand.

// *what about my birthday?I only wanted to spend it with you.*
-nathalie kristine

I wanted this to last

Can you please tell me,
what was it that caused our downfall?
Was it because I gave my everything into healing you,
when I was broken myself?
It could've been your inability to display emotion,
or maybe it was my inability to control mine.

Or was it simply because,
we were too young to realize what we had.
We both just weren't ready.

Maybe we were perfect for each other,
but timing was not on our side.

// were you the right person, just wrong time?
    -nathalie kristine

denial

I wanted this to last, I know you did too,
so why didn't you stay?

Did all of our promises mean nothing?
I didn't give up on us,
at least not yet.

// why didn't our relationship last
if we both wanted it too?
*   -nathalie kristine*

I wanted this to last

I wanted you to fight for me,
as horrible as it sounds.

I didn't feel loved,
not until I threatened to walk away,
and you would beg me to stay.

I thought you would have tried a little harder,
or stayed just a little bit longer,
 just long enough to say goodbye.

// why didn't you at least say goodbye?
-nathalie kristine

denial

I thought you wanted love like this,
You said you wanted all of me.

You said you'd never hurt me.
You said you'd be here for me.
You said you'd never leave me.

Well you left,
you destroyed me.
why do you claim to still love me?

// where's the man I once knew?
-nathalie kristine

I wanted this to last

You are not a man of your word.

Sometimes I wonder how disappointed
your past self would be, if he ever knew that
you didn't keep the promises he made me.

// where's the man I once knew?
-nathalie kristine

denial

I will wait for you,
I am not sure for how long.
I will wait until I cannot remember you anymore.

Maybe I will end up waiting forever,
or maybe I will give up too early.

What if I decide to let you go,
and you decide come back?
Or what if you never do,
and I spend my whole life waiting for you.

// what if I waste my entire life waiting for you?
   -nathalie kristine

I wanted this to last

Please tell me I'm not as forgettable
as your silence is making it seem.

// have you already forgotten me?
  -nathalie kristine

denial

I have clung onto to your identity as if it were my own.
I have fallen in love with all the things you used to love,
just because it reminded me of you.
I started traveling to the places you used to always mention,
and listening to the music I used to always say I hated.

I have become a reflection of who you used to be,
in an awful attempt to keep the memory of you close to me.

Time has passed and your absence grown more apparent,
and the only thing I have done,
is drive myself further away from my own identity.

I have lost myself holding onto the ghost of you.

// I don't even know who I am anymore.
    -nathalie kristine

I wanted this to last

I'm haunted by your promises,
the ones you never kept.

// why did you make promises you knew you couldn't keep.
-nathalie kristine

denial

You never told me you didn't love me,
or that we were over,
you never even said goodbye,
I just need some closure.
You left all our strings still attached,
so now a part of me believes you are planning to come back.

Tell me my love is it true?
you know that I would wait for you,
forever if I had too.

// I can't let go of you.
-nathalie kristine

I wanted this to last

In my head it is still July,
and I still live at my mother's house,
I'll soon hear a knock on my door.

In reality it's December,
and it's been months since I moved out,
I can hardly remember the last time
I was at my mother's house.

I thought it would get easier.
But as each day passes,
instead of growing accustomed to your absence,
the hole in my heart lingers for you more.

Maybe it's because I never got to tell you goodbye,
If only you knew about all the times I've cried.

// my brain is still convinced it's July.
 -nathalie kristine

denial

I don't know if I will ever be able to accept how things ended.
I fear acceptance.
If I accept that you are no longer mine,
and I am no longer yours,
I will forget you.

Our memories will slowly become replaced,
and the days we spent together will fade away,
somewhere unaccessible in my mind.
I fear that I will not be able to recall
what it felt like to kiss you.

I will forget the sound of your voice
when you would whisper " I love you."
Or how it felt every time I rested my head
on your chest.

I don't want to forget you.

I'd rather wallow in our memories forever than
forget the comfort we brought each other.

// I don't want to let myself forget you.
-nathalie kristine

I wanted this to last

Why didn't want it to work with the girl
who loved you enough to understand you?

Do you know how much love it takes?
to try and understand someone,
even while they are hurting you?

// I was hurting myself more trying to understand you.
  -nathalie kristine

denial

Before I completely let you go,
you won't miss me, right?

// maybe you will miss me, but just not enough.
         -nathalie kristine

i wanted this to last

I never got to tell your sister how proud I was
of seeing her grow,
or how much your mother inspires me,
I guess she'll never know.

You didn't just leave me when you walked away,
you left me with so many things I never got to say,
not only to you but to all your family members
that I also loved for a short time too.

// my mother still talks about you.
   -nathalie kristine

denial

My mind is stuck in a constant state of nostalgia,
In my head it is still July.
The birds are chirping outside your window,
while my head is resting on your pillow.

In my head it's July,
we have plans to watch the sunrise.
nothing yet has been tainted,
not an ounce of our love has been wasted.

I catch a glimpse of outside my window,
I don't know what I was expecting to see,
but it wasn't all this snow.
The realization is something,
I don't want to know.

Don't tell me it's not July,
and we no longer speak;
the very thought of all our memories,
makes my body weak.
I feel the ache of nostalgia coursing through my bones,
this is a type of pain I have never known.
I can feel my insides rotting,
not accepting passing time.

don't tell me that it's March now, and I am all alone.
Time has surely passed us by,
yet somehow my mind has been convinced,
that it is still July.

// in my head I'm happy living in a lie.
  -nathalie kristine

I wanted this to last

I don't think our past selves would be happy
with how we let things end.

// oh how disappointed they'd be.
 -nathalie kristine

denial

what do I do if my entire life I cannot forget you?
I know I will find another to love me,
but my heart will always belong to you.
he might pick me flowers,
or carry me when I feel weak,
But my mind will constantly remember,
who we used to be.

either I end up alone,
to forever wallow in old memories;
Or I let another fall in love with me,
knowing I can never fully love them,
not to the same extent I loved you.

How am I supposed to live knowing you never
got to experience the rest of the love I had to give?

I don't know if my heart will ever truly let you go,
There's just too many things you never got to know.

// have you already let go of me?
  -nathalie kristine

I wanted this to last

I wasn't ready to let things end,
How did you so easily let go?

I'm still not ready to say goodbye.
Does that mean anything?
Do I mean anything?
Am I nothing?
maybe I was always nothing.

don't tell me please,
I am not ready to hear the confirmation,
of everything I fear.

// maybe I never meant anything to you.
　-nathalie kristine

denial

" I'll talk to you when I'm ready"

It has been 2 months.
You still haven't talked to me.
You're never going to be ready are you?

You'll never explain where I went wrong,
and I doubt you'll ever respond to my letters.
Am I just never going to get an answer?

Maybe I will keep waiting,
just a little bit longer.

I am becoming angry with your silence.
You are slowly killing me.

// why do you avoid a conversation with me?
-nathalie kristine

anger

anger

Never to be loved the way I love.

I hate love, all it's ever done is destroy me.
When will I be taken care of, in the same ways I care of?
Will anyone ever notice the little things about me,
like I notice all of theirs?
When will someone make me feel understood,
like the way I try to understand?
Will anyone ever love me for who I actually am?
Or am I just meant to be alone?
Will I ever be loved the way I love?

What if the only way I'll ever receive the love I give,
is by giving it to myself?

// why has nobody ever loved me how I've loved them?
-nathalie kristine

I wanted this to last

Why don't you tell them how much
of myself I gave loving you?

Why don't you tell them how I spent every night
writing you letters, knowing you might even
never care enough to read them?

Why don't you tell them how
I would pray to God just to talk to him about you,
and ask him to watch over you?

But instead,
You tell everyone I was crazy,
& how I never did anything right.

One day you'll see how much I gave and how much I loved,
and you'll regret treating me the way you did.

// you painted me as a villain, when all I wanted was love.
-nathalie kristine

anger

I hate that I am weak for you.
I hate that you are the only person that has ever convinced me
to break all the promises I made to myself.
You take advantage of me so easily,
and I let you.

But if it were anyone else, their hands wouldn't
have made it anywhere near my body.
You knew about the parts of myself
 I was saving to give away to you.
 You told me I was more than just an object to you.

Yet still,
you take me to your bed, and I fall for your lie
that you won't break my boundaries.
You wait until you know I'm drunk,
 just so you can kiss me,
And pretend as if you still love me
 I fall for it all.

You stole parts of me I promised
I'd keep safe for my husband.

The husband you were supposed to be.

// you were supposed to protect my purity, not ruin it.
-nathalie kristine

I wanted this to last

you took parts of me
you never deserved to have.

You waited to have sex with me our whole relationship,
But when we were no longer together
that's all you wanted me for.

It doesn't make any fucking sense.

// why did you use me?
-nathalie kristine

anger

August 20th.
You know the night you fucked her I knew.

I don't know how but It was a haunting feeling,
More than just stomach drop,
it was as if my lungs stopped working.
My heart quit beating,
and my hands began shaking.
I knew deep in my heart,
 it was the gut feeling of betrayal.

I pretended as if it were nothing,
but my insides felt sick with disgust.
I want to know how.
how did you fuck her, knowing it would kill me?

How did you give away the purity we promised
 each other so easily?

How did you do it with no remorse?

// I was saving my body for you.
  -nathalie kristine

I wanted this to last

Do you even regret what you did to me?
Do you even feel any remorse?

How could you be so proud, so cocky,
to fuck someone else so easily.
When I saved every inch of my body for you.
for a man who gave his away,
as if sex meant nothing, and our promises never mattered.
the most intimate way to know someone,
was all worth it for her.

Tell me why I still save my body for a man
who couldn't save himself for me?

// I don't understand why I still think I'll marry you.
    -nathalie kristine

anger

I hope you never feel the type of pain I felt.
the type of pain that makes it agonizing
every time you catch a glimpse into a mirror.
I'd stare for hours picking apart every piece of myself,
wondering if I'd ever be enough for anyone.

I hope that you never feel the type of pain that
makes your stomach turn inside itself,
It will attempt to puke out all of the sadness you have felt.

The type of pain that makes your heart hurt so badly,
you bruise your skin while trying to console it.
But no amount of grasping at your chest,
will stop the aching pit.

I hope you never feel the type of pain so strong,
you stare blankly at the bottle of pills in front of you,
trying to come up with one reason
not to take them all.

The type of pain where you have to hold back your tears,
when you get a glance at two strangers,
who are so deeply in love.
It's not fair to have see strangers enjoying the very thing
we've always dreamed of.

I hope you never feel the type of pain that
stops your lungs from working, I'd gasp for air in between
sobs, but I couldn't get myself to breathe.

I hope you never feel the type of pain I felt.
But what I do hope,
is that you somehow understand it.
That some deep part of you realizes,
how much pain you put me through when
you claimed to love me.

I hope you feel the type of pain
that leaves you with regret in your throat.
The painful regret of words you never spoke,
The type of pain that makes you decide to change.

// I wish you knew how much I suffered because of you.
-nathalie kristine

anger

I'll never truly be able to forget you.
No matter how years pass,
or how many memories of ours get replaced,
you are now a permanent part of my brain.

I hate it.

I wish I could erase every memory,
and any last thought of you.

you don't deserve to be a
permanent part of my mind.

// how do I make myself forget you?
-nathalie kristine

I wanted this to last

I don't understand.
How could someone who has claimed to love me,
leave me with no answer?
How could you let me beg just for a simple explanation,
while you enjoy my suffering?

I sat next to you in your car and we talked about our future,
you spoke about it like it was guaranteed to me.
We talked about the parts of ourselves we would
work on for the next two weeks.
You let me believe we weren't over,
and you sealed it with a promise.
You told me we would talk again after just two weeks.

more than two weeks have passed,
and you haven't talked to me.
I have begged you for any sort of explanation,
Or just a simple response,
but you given me none.

I kept my promise.
I got better for you.
If you don't love me anymore
why don't you just tell me?

Your silence is more painful than
anything you could ever say.

// I was so excited to show you how much I improved.
-nathalie kristine

anger

I thought you were a person I understood,
but I fear that I never once did.
If only I had known about the heartless side you hid.

How did you so easily betray all
the loving words you used to say?
I don't think I recognize you.

// you have become someone I never knew.
   -nathalie kristine

i wanted this to last

You never even said sorry.
Your apologies were forced by me.
I sat on your bedside, tears running down my face,
begging for you to feel an ounce of remorse.
I begged you to apologize for the pain you put me in.

Maybe if you were sorry, it would console
the agony I felt inside.

" what do you want me to say to you.. "
That is all you could come up with.

I wanted you to tell me that you were sorry for choosing
to hurt the person that you promised to love.
You looked me in the eyes, and pulled me close
into your chest and said;
nothing.

Maybe that was just your way of saying sorry,
Or so I tell myself.

I wanted so badly to hate you for saying nothing to me,
but the feeling of being close enough
to hear your heart beating,
brought me a type of comfort I wish it didn't.

I let myself be consoled by the comfort of your presence,
instead of the knowledge of your remorse.

I hope one day I get an apology
for everything you put me through.

// you were never sorry for the suffering you caused me.
-nathalie kristine

anger

I don't blame you for not loving me,
I blame you for pretending that you did.
My pain was never caused by unrequited love,
it was caused by your sick selfishness of
loving how much I loved you.

You enjoyed how I fed your ego,
you were the only exception,
to all the rules and promises I made to myself.
You loved all the power I gave to you,
and how taking advantage of me was so easy too.

You don't love me,
But you led to me believe you still did,
it was so much deeper than just unrequited love.

breaking me apart put you together.

*// maybe for a short a time you actually did love me,
  but you don't anymore.*

-nathalie kristine

Time heals all wounds.

Or so they tell you,
but the horrible truth that I have learned is,
time heals nothing.

The pain just becomes so familiar until
you don't feel it anymore.
There are things that happened in my childhood,
I have not healed from.
The pain of it has only been drowned out.
but I have not healed,
In reality,
it is the very cause of the wounds I have now.

Time heals nothing.
It only creates new wounds to sorrow over,
each being deeper than the last.

// I thought by now I'd feel better.
   -nathalie kristine

anger

Its not fair.
It's not fair at all.

I never got an apology,
I never got an explanation.
So why did I go out of my way to give you one?
I apologized for things that weren't my fault.
I gave you explanations that you never deserved.

So wheres my apology?
Wheres is my explanation?

Its not fair that I am expected to move on without
any explanation or apology.
I made it easier for you, you only made it harder for me.
Nothing about love has ever been fair for me.

// I regret the apologies I gave you.
   -nathalie kristine

I wanted this to last

I hope you are haunted by thoughts of
what we could have been.

The places we would have gone,
the family we would have had,
all the memories we could have made,
The camping trips we would have taken,
or the summer nights we could have spent.

The house we almost moved into,
and that scrapbook we could have finished,
all the flowers you could have picked me,
and the ring you almost gave me,
The future we almost had.

// I hope you are haunted by what we almost had.
-nathalie kristine

anger

What is so wrong with me that made you decide to give up?
So fucking easy too,
as if I was a person that never even mattered to you.
You did it without even thinking twice or even telling me.
You kept me in limbo.

What did I even do wrong?
how do you so easily ignore all my calls?
Are we were ever going to talk?
You promised we were going to.

Well, I never got an answer,
and here I am 6 months later, still fucking wondering.

// I hate that you never gave me an answer.
-nathalie kristine

I wanted this to last

I think what I am most angry about is
that you were the one who hurt me,
so why I am the only one who suffers.

You get to move on with your life,
and fall asleep at night, while I lie awake.
begging to God for any sort of answer,
to feel okay enough to be able to sleep.

You wake up every morning and I don't cross your mind,
when the thought of you has never left mine.
When I wake up the sadness overwhelms me.
I have to remind myself how to breathe,
I have to push away my pain and pretend like
I don't feel it.

While you get to move on as if nothing happened.
That is what I am most angry about.

// If only you understood my suffering.
-Nathalie Kristine

anger

I was looking back on our pictures,
when I realized there is not a single
 photo that I am not smiling in.
you truly did make me the happiest
 I have ever been.

No matter how many good things that
 have happened in my life since then,
I still have never smiled like the way I did
when I was with you.

I don't know if I am grateful or spiteful about it.
you made me the happiest I have ever been,
but only to take it all away.
You always knew you weren't gonna stay.

I hope I smile like the way I used to
but without you someday.

// I miss my bright smile.
-nathalie kristine

I wanted this to last

I am filled with so much anger.
The anger is burning me from the inside out,
it boils and bubbles up until it reaches the edges of my mouth.
If only I could yell and scream all the bitterness out.

I wish you understood how angry you make me.
I want to claw my brain out every time I think of you.
It sickens me how much I still love you,

after how much you took from me,
how horrible you treated me,
how easily you replaced me,
after all the times you showed me
 that you don't care.

I hate myself for still loving you,
 despite all you put me through.

*// I want to pull you close to me
 then whisper that I hate you.*
-nathalie kristine

anger

I want the most hurtful things to fall out of my lips,
I want to say horrible things to hurt you,
 in the same way you hurt me.
I want you sit there and have to look at me,
not knowing who I am anymore.

You'll look me in the eyes and question
if I ever even loved you at all.
I want to use all your weaknesses against you,
So you suffer the way you made me suffer.
I want you to feel the same pain that you caused me,
but not because I actually want you to suffer.
But because one day,
I want you to finally understand everything I went through
just because
I chose to love you.

// I just want my pain to be understood.
-nathalie kristine

I wanted this to last

If I had the chance to erase every memory of you,
Good and bad,
I would.

I would do it without even thinking twice,
or even looking back.
You have no business being in my memory.

If only I could erase everything
 that had to do with you.

//please get the fuck out of my mind.
-nathalie kristine

anger

Do you whisper to her with the same soft voice,
saying that you love her, right before she falls asleep,
just like how you used to always tell me?
Do you write her love letters,
like the ones I used to write to you?

Do you call her beautiful and pretend that it's her name,
like you used to do with me?

Do you stop the car just to pick her flowers too?
does she keep every one of them
as if they were worth more than gold,
like I used too?

So tell me,
Do you love her in all the ways,
that I used to beg you?

// I wonder if she gets everything I wanted from you. .
-nathalie kristine

I wanted this to last

You are a liar.
You make up stories to cover up the mistakes you made,
You paint me to be someone I never was.

Do you lie to convince other people I am bad,
or do you lie only to try to convince yourself of that?
or maybe you lie to avoid the weight of your own regret.

I have dealt with my regret.
I have let the regret of my mistakes sink into my chest,
and I have cried so many tears just wishing
for a way to go back to fix the things that should
have never been broken.
There is no going back, there is only forward.
I have let the weight of my regret,
change me for the better.
I will never make the same mistakes again.

You have run from your regret,
but it will catch up to you
and the weight of your regret,

will eat you alive from the inside.

// you can't lie to yourself forever.
   -nathalie kristine

anger

You will never have to hurt the way I do,
and because of that I hate you.
You will never understand what its like to know
the person you loved more than yourself,
the person you planned your future with,
just doesn't love you anymore.
But for some reason,
they can't look you in the eyes and say it to you.

You will never know what it's like to be strung along
on crumbs of useless hope,
lying to yourself that they still love you,
even though they keep hurting you.

You will never understand what its like to sob on the
bathroom floor wanting nothing but
an answer, or a simple explanation,
something that would make sense to ease the ache.
You will never know sadness so deep,
you can feel it physically.
You will never have to hurt the way I do,
I would never hurt you in the same ways you have hurt me.
I hate that you get away with the pain you caused me.
You get to move on,
while I am left in the dark,
With no response.

I hate you.

// i wish you could feel the sadness I felt.
   -nathalie kristine

I wanted this to last

You have ruined my perspective on love.

It would have been easier for me
if you just told me you didn't love me anymore.
But you didn't. You continuously feed me lies.
When you really loved me,
you would bring me flowers, and wipe away my tears,
get me out of bed to make dinner as we danced,
You would protect my boundaries,
and waited to have sex.

You were everything I hoped love would be,
back when I thought you loved me.
how do you ever expect me to trust anyone
when everything you did for me was all for nothing?

Every time you squeezed my hand three times
to let me know you loved me,
Every kiss at the door
Every "I love you"
Every promise that was supposed to be kept,
none of it meant anything to you.

If a man ever loves me in the same ways
that you used too,
It will only cause me pain,
reminding me of you.

You have ruined my perception of love.

//why couldn't you have just been more awful to me
-nathalie kristine

anger

I'll tear all the pieces of you out of my brain until the day
I can no longer remember your name.

When the time comes along and I have finally moved on,
I won't remember the way we used to dance in my kitchen,
and I'll have ripped up all the notes we had written.

I won't remember the sound of your laugh,
and I'll have burned all of our photographs.

There will come a time when I can no longer recall
how you made me feel so easily forgotten after it all.
Or the nights I spent crying on my bathroom floor,
begging you to stay just a second more.

I'll convince myself that you never existed,
pretending my life won't be forever afflicted.

// I can't wait for the day when your name has no meaning
-nathalie kristine

I wanted this to last

They say that love is a choice,
but if that were true I would have never chosen to love you.

I knew we wouldn't last from the moment we met,
deep down you knew it too.
So tell me why my heart aches for you,
if our end was something we always knew.
Why, after 8 months with no signs of you, and knowing
you've moved on, why is my heart still longing
just to be in your presence?
How is it even possible to still feel this type of ache for you?

If love was really a choice I wouldn't choose
to continue to love you,
not after everything you've put me through.

// I didn't choose to love you.
-nathalie kristine

anger

You left without saying anything, and I don't understand why.
Was it because you planned to take
all the good parts of me with you?
You took my motivation,
my happiness,
my future,
my comfort.
You robbed me of all my good qualities.

The only thing you left me with was my pain.
Pain that fueled my anger, not towards you,
but towards myself.
I blamed everything on me,
It was my fault you left.
if only I had been a little bit prettier,
If only I had given you my body,
or maybe I was too annoying,
if only I wasn't so emotional,
or my brain wasn't so black and white.
If I only I had told you about the suffering I felt.

I have nothing but anger toward myself.

I started to use the pills I always told you not to take.
I drink until I can no longer remember anymore ,
It's been so long one since I've eaten
my hunger is easy too ignore.

You have no idea how much you affected me,
I'm no longer the girl I used to be.

// I wonder if you'd like the person losing you has turned me into.
-nathalie kristine

I wanted this to last

I know you.

I know the anger you hold towards me,
stems from all the sadness I caused you.
you act as if you are angry at the whole world,
but in fact, it is quite the contrary.

Anger is a secondary emotion to pain.
You choose to mask your grief with anger.
I know you're not really angry.
You just don't know how to handle your own pain
so you turn it into anger,

an emotion you are far too familiar with.

// I guess I'm not actually angry at you either.
  -nathalie kristine

anger

I want to stop loving the people that hurt me.
I want to stop trying to understand their pain,
more than my own.
I don't want to forgive you for anything,
but I do.
I forgive you.

If only I could hate you,
just as much as I love you.

// you are only hurting me because you are in pain too.
-nathalie kristine

I wanted this to last

Why have I let myself be consoled by
the comfort of your presence,
instead of the knowledge of your remorse?

/ I hate that I forgive you.
　-nathalie kristine

bargaining

I wanted this to last

Behind your sweet blue eyes,
I see all the tears you have cried,
for they have left stains on your cheeks.

I can tell that you hide all your emotions inside,
because you are afraid to look weak.

Only, they will never subside,
no matter how hard you may try,
and suppression will cause it to leak.

Please don't hold them aside,
In my arms you can cry,
I promise I will not call you weak.

Even after our separation
I hope you can see,
all your silent desperation,
has never been quiet to me.

// and it never will be
-nathalie kristine

bargaining

Please just take me with you
I don't care if our love is doomed,
I have only ever wanted you.

Please just take me with you,
you're the only one that comforts my wounds,
I already know our love is doomed.

// we didn't have enough time together.
-nathalie kristine

I wanted this to last

378 letters.
I counted them before I handed you the notebook.
That's how many letters I wrote to you, with each letter
I poured pieces of myself onto each page in hopes that one day
you'd read them and understand. That one day you'd read that
notebook and finally know how much I was suffering in ways
I couldn't bring myself to ever say out loud.
You'd read all the pages filled with poems and reasons why I
loved you, and you'd finally know how much I appreciated
you for who you were.
I handed you the notebook with all 378 letters,
and you gave me one lifeless look with just a single
tear in your eye,
Yet you still said nothing.

maybe you'll never read my letters,
maybe I just wasted so many precious words on a boy
who never actually loved me enough to understand.
Maybe my letters will sit and rot inside that notebook until one
day it just gets tossed away, never to read by you.

Or maybe one day you will read them.
You'll find the notebook shoved away
in a spot you had long forgotten,
You'll open the pages and
start to realize how much you hurt me.

With each letter, you'll begin to understand,
what I begged for so long to be understood.

But by that time it will be too late.
And I'll have begun writing letters to someone else.

// will you ever read everything I wrote you?
  -nathalie kristine

bargaining

Maybe one conversation could fix it all.

We could talk about where we both went wrong,
and come up with solutions to all the silly issues
that now seem so small.
You could tell me about all the feelings you used to ignore,
and I won't be afraid to admit my own suffering anymore.

We can exchange stories of the pain we went through,
to reach a new level of understanding,
one we've never had before.

Instead of suppressing your emotions,
you can finally let yourself feel them,
all the months of absence from each other
would be for a good reason.

At the end of the conversation,
we will both have grown so much closer.

Maybe just one conversation
and we could start over.

//what if we had just one last conversation?
  -nathalie kristine

I wanted this to last

You've left me with nothing to hold onto,
Yet still,
 I grasp my hands around a void.
I claim to feel something,
but I am holding onto nothing.

I tell myself you'll be back,
attempting to console the wound you caused.
I know deep down you're gone,
but my heart has no regard.

I will continue to grasp my hands around thin air,
hoping one day your hands will be there.

// tell me are you going to come back?
-nathalie kristine

bargaining

I wish you knew how sorry I was Isaac.

There's not a day that goes by where I don't regret
the end of our relationship, but I did keep all my promises.
I only wanted to be better for you.
and I did, I got better.
I found out I have a trauma-caused mental disorder,
now it all makes sense.
I'm sorry for what I put you through, without even realizing it.
I wish I would've known the way I felt inside my head was
caused by a mental illness. If only I had known.
Maybe I could have prevented the hurt
we both caused each other.
I feel like I failed in a lot of ways I wish I didn't.
I miss you.
I'm still in love with you even though I wish I wasn't.
I hope one day our paths cross,
and we get to fall in love all over again.
But next time, we'll get the happy ending we always wanted.

no one will ever mean to me as much as you my love.

// if only I could go back in time.
-nathalie kristine

I wanted this to last

The only time I ever felt the love I begged for
was when you thought I was going to leave.
    I see now that we both grew tired of it.

You grew tired of me constantly pulling away,
and I grew tired of only feeling loved,
when you'd beg me to stay.

I can see now where I went wrong,
but now it's too late,
and we're both gone.

// we both drained each other without even realizing it.
    -nathalie kristine

bargaining

You were my first love.
You got the very best of me and now,
I will never love another how I loved you.

// you are the person behind my poetry.
　　-nathalie kristine

I wanted this to last

Why can't I just get an explanation from you?
My mind is in a state of constant utter torture.

Your actions betray the loving words you say,
If only you would tell me you hate me.

At least then it would all make sense,
and my heart would stop making excuses for you.

// but until then I can't blame you.
  -nathalie kristine

bargaining

We can still start over, it's not too late.
You can pretend like you don't know my name,
and I'll pretend like I don't know yours.

You'll ask me how I pronounce it,
and I'll notice your slight smile.
I'll ask what yours is as I'll pretend that
hearing your name again doesn't sting.

we'd look at each and laugh,
neither of us is very good at pretending.

We could still start over,
if only you would ask.

// only you might never ask me that.
  -nathalie kristine

I wanted this to last

I would give anything to have a time machine.

I would go back to the night of August 1st,
just to turn my car around.
I'd run back into your room, where you'd be sleeping in
your bed, I'd crawl right into your arms
and my lay head against your chest.
I would whisper to you

" please don't let me go."

You'll ask me what had happened,
and I'll answer

" you don't ever need to know."

// If only I had turned my car around.
   -nathalie kristine

bargaining

" Everything is fixable."

// I wish I would've listened.
　-nathalie kristine

I wanted this to last

If only I had realized sooner.

If only I had realized my own faults,
If only I had told you the things I was too afraid to say.
If only I let you in on the vulnerable parts of me.
If only you'd stayed.

Things would have been so different.

// I wish I just had known.
-nathalie kristine

bargaining

I hope you know we could always start over,
despite all the suffering we have both felt.

Even though we are apart, we suffer together.
We also build strength,
we also push through,
we learn about losing each other,
together.

Although we are far apart
we've been through it all together.

We suffer under the same sky,
and cry out to the same moon.

I hope our paths cross again,
maybe we can teach each other what we have learned.

// I have learned a lot from losing you
   V-nathalie saldana

I wanted this to last

We almost made it
We should have.

We were so close,
You had me bought me a ring,
You only showed it to me after things had ended.
but my God,
It was the most beautiful ring I have ever seen.

The way it sparkled,
The gold band.
It was the exact ring I had dreamed of since I was a little girl.

We almost had forever together.
Almost.

// why did you show me the ring?
-nathalie kristine

bargaining

I hope you know how sorry I am.
even though I am angry about how you treated me,
I know I wasn't perfect either.

I made mistakes,
and so did you.
I caused you pain,
and you caused me pain too.
I didn't understand,
and neither did you.

We kept hurting each other hoping
that we would understand how it felt.
We were both naive.

I'm sorry for the pain I caused you because
of the pain I was in myself.
and I forgive you for the hurt you caused me
because of the suffering you felt.

// I'm sorry.
-nathalie kristine

I wanted this to last

Last night I knew exactly what to say,
but you weren't around to hear it.

I tried to call but you didn't pick up,
I sent you a text that will never deliver,
I wrote you a letter that you will probably never read.

If only you'd hear what I had to say,
Maybe it wouldn't change anything,
but what if it could?

// will you ever answer me?
-nathalie kristine

bargaining

I dreamed of summer last night,
If only I could live in my dreams.

I hope that one day I wake up back in July,
The sun will be shining on our faces as we give each other
our groggy good-morning kisses.
We'll get out of bed to make breakfast together while
we make plans for our summer day.

Maybe today we can go to the flower field,
the one I had always talked about going to.
Maybe you'll finally take me there,
like you had planned to.

I hope I wake up back in July.

// my dreams are just a lie.
-nathalie kristine

I wanted this to last

Sometimes I picture the happy life we used to
always talk about living.

Maybe in another timeline,
we are living what we used to talk about.

// do you think about our plans too?
　-nathalie kristine

bargaining

The ache to go back is something I dont think
I will ever stop feeling.

If only I could turn back time but keep my knowledge,
I could have prevented so many things.

If only there was a way to go back,
and save what we used to have.

// you will always be a memory I'd die to relive.
*   -nathalie kristine*

I wanted this to last

I stare at our pictures for hours on end,
reliving the moments we had in my head.
The nostalgia overwhelms me, I can remember
every moment as if it had just happened.

6 months.

It's been over 6 months since I have been with you.
why does it feel like it was just yesterday when I'd run to greet
you at the door and jump in your arms?

How is it possible to remember our moments so vividly,
when I know they have faded from your memory.

// do you still remember little things about me?
  -nathalie kristine

bargaining

Was there something I could have done?

Is there anything I could have said,
that would of have kept you from giving up?

// is there anything I can still do?
  -nathalie kristine

I wanted this to last

The silence of unspoken words,
 a sound that aches to be heard.
All the things you left unsaid,
they will take over your head.

I can no longer sleep, If only we could speak.
This feeling of regret, my mind cannot forget.

all the words I never got to say,
they haven't gone away.

// I still have so much left to say.
  -nathalie kristine

bargaining

I love you still,
please just come back.

We can still live out the life we always wanted.

// I still remember our plans for our mountain house.
  -nathalie kristine

I wanted this to last

I think maybe if I understood how you became so cold,
I wouldn't be so bitter.
Can you just explain it to me?
Why haven't you called?

You promised me.
How did you break your promises so easily?
I just want things to make sense in my head.
Why is it so hard for you to give me an answer?
I just want to understand.

// I don't fear rejection, I fear my own ignorance.
  -nathalie kristine

bargaining

Thank you for being there when no one else was,
you stayed longer than anyone ever has.

But in the end, you still fucking left too.
I just wish I could blame you.

// why was it so easy to leave me?
-nathalie kristine

I wanted this to last

Do you still remember the sound of my voice,
like I remember yours?
Do you still remember the nights we stayed up late
talking about anything?
or have you already forgotten everything,
I will always remember?

Please tell me you remember me,
I will always remember you.

I don't want to be forgotten by the person,
I will remember most.

// I won't forget you.
-nathalie kristine

bargaining

In the meantime I'll be looking for you at every stoplight,
hoping that the car that stops next to me,
might one day be yours.

I look for you every time I pass by the places
we always used to go, sometimes I wonder
if you ever look for me.

maybe one day we will run into each other,
and reminisce on how things used to be.

// I still drive down the street you used to live on
               -nathalie kristine

I wanted this to last

All I ever wanted was to make you proud,
Why could never see?

I know it's been so long,
but please just tell me
are you proud of me?

No matter how much pain you've caused me,
I have still pushed through.
and even after it all,
I would still choose to love you.

// this poem isn't just about you.
-nathalie kristine

bargaining

If I had a chance to speak to you again,
I am not sure what I would tell you.

There is both too much to explain,
and nothing else left to say.

// I wonder what you would have to say.
  -nathalie kristine

depression

depression

The sadness is comforting,
a comfort I never thought I would return to,
yet here I am again.

broken by another boy I thought was different.
it's true when they say life will teach you the
same lesson over and over until you learn.

I guess some things I'll never learn,
the one I love will always be worth the pain to me.

// loving you was still worth all the pain you caused me.
-nathalie kristine

I wanted this to last

I want to hate you I really do,
but my heart cannot stop loving you
my sadness is so deep,
I can feel it physically.
you have no idea of all the agony,
you chose to put me through.

I have sobbed for hours clawing my hand over my chest,
laying on my bathroom floor.
I don't want to feel this way anymore.
I have tried everything to console the pain I am in.
But my pain cannot be consoled.
It doesn't care how many tears I already cried,
It doesn't go away,
no matter how hard I try.

I wake up with bruises on my chest,
they are from my own hands.
I hurt myself by trying too hard to console the pain I felt.

// I can only blame myself.
  -nathalie kristine

depression

Nothing could have ever prepared me for the type of hurt
I went through when I had to walk away.

// I never wanted things to end.
-nathalie kristine

You may have never told me,
but it was your actions that screamed at me.
You don't love me anymore.

I don't know why, but you just don't.

When you loved me you were there.
you were there knocking on my doorstep,
you didn't stop knocking until I answered.

Now I am here knocking on your doorstep,
the only difference is you never answered.

I kept knocking hoping just for a reply,
but instead, you laugh at me.
You tell everyone how pathetic and crazy I am
for knocking at your door.

So why does my heart still wait for you to answer?

*// my heart won't let you go until
you tell me what I already know.
-nathalie kristine*

depression

The emptiness is still there,
the emptiness of the girl I used to be.
Ripped away by someone who couldn't have cared less.
I had so much care and hope for the world,
and now
I am heartless.

// the emptiness will never leave.
-nathalie kristine

I miss you.
Or maybe I don't actually miss you,
maybe I just miss the potential of who you could have been,
or who you pretended to be.

The boy I locked eyes with from across the crowded room
was no longer a bright blissful blue,
But instead, they were a dull pale version.
You didn't look like you.

You held a cigarette in your hand as if it was
the most important thing to exist.
It seems you have forgotten about the days,
when you worked so hard to quit.
Maybe I don't miss you,
maybe I just miss a version of you
that no longer exists,
Or maybe it never actually did.

// I miss the sweet boy I thought you were.
 -nathalie kristine

depression

My sadness has begun to consume me.
I try to leave the sadness but I have become attached to it.
If I still feel sad over you,
there's a possibility you might feel sad too.
I don't want you to feel sadness,
but knowing that there's a chance you might feel
anything towards me,

is comforting in the most dreadful way.

// I can't explain the sadness.
-nathalie kristine

I wanted this to last

I feel like there is no reason to continue.

But even though I don't want too,
my heart keeps beating,
my lungs keep breathing,
and my eyes do not cry forever.

My body keeps me alive,
even though my soul aches to die.

// I don't want to experience life.
Bbbbb-nathalie kristine

depression

You left a bottle of your cologne in my bedroom,
sometimes I'll spray it on my pillow,
and as close my eyes to sleep,
I pretend as if I am laying on your chest again.
your warm chest was the most comforting place
that I have ever known.

I don't want to run out of your cologne.

// I miss my spot on your chest .
-nathalie kristine

Maybe it is just impossible to love me.

I am too hard to understand.
my brain is a mess,
no one could even begin to try and comprehend.

What if I'm just meant to be
 alone in the end?

// I wish I understood my own mind.
-nathalie kristine

depression

Things can never go back to the way they used to be.
I tell myself that it could also mean that things
can be better than they ever were.
But that is a silly excuse for the ugly truth,
that the way I view you will never be
as sweet as it once was.

I can never think of you as someone
who could never hurt me,
because you already have.

And although I forgive you,
the way I view you has been tainted.
I will never be able to look at you
 in the same way I used to.

We can never go back to what once was.

// I've only just realized you're gone.
-nathalie kristine

I wanted this to last

I have begged every man in my life to love me,
even my own fucking father.

I would sit and cry just asking why he didn't love me
anymore. I was just 7 years old, dying to understand why the
man that was supposed to show me what love was like,
made me feel like it didn't even exist.
We used to spend every second together.
I'd come with him to work, and draw him pictures during all
his meetings, until one day he just stopped caring.
I can remember sobbing because he'd never answer my calls,
and some days he just wouldn't come home.
I'd miss my father so much I would sleep wearing his shirts
because they smelt just like him, and it was the only thing
that brought me some sort of comfort.
For the next 11 years,
the men in my life would continue to
show me everything love was not.
Then I met you.
you changed everything for me for so long.
You showed me everything that love was supposed to be,
you showed up for me in ways nobody ever has.
until one day,
you became just like my father,
And without any explanation you just stopped caring.
I may have been 20 years old nonstop texting you, calling you,
but in reality, I was the same 7-year-old girl trying to
understand why the man that claimed to love me,
just disappeared.

You cut the same wound in my heart my father
had already made.

// I now sleep with your sweater
just like how I'd sleep with my father's shirt.
-nathalie kristine

depression

I am in love with someone who no longer exists,
you are not the person my heart aches for.

To successfully grieve the death of who you once were,
I cannot be haunted by the ghost of the person you are now.
Please let me grieve you in peace,
and do not give me false hopes that the boy I love still exists.

He will never exist again.

// you only exist in my memory
-nathalie kristine

Maybe I deserve someone else but I always wanted you.
It hurts to think that one day you'll decide to be
the person that I deserved.
And although by then I may have found
someone else who fulfills that role,
there will always that gaping hole.

a permanent void in my heart,
the result of a first's love destruction.

// I wanted to belong to you.
-nathalie kristine

depression

I hate you for everything that you have done,
but I still love you for who you used to be.

// the sweet boy that still lives in my memory.
-nathalie kristine

I wanted this to last

It feels like something is rotting inside my heart
and if I don't claw it out,
my heart will decay.

I wish I could rip my heart out from inside my body,
to save myself from all this suffering.

// I want to feel nothing.
-nathalie kristine

depression

I've noticed you've found someone new,
though I try to look away, I can't help but see
the way you smile at her with such ease,
the way you touch her, it brings me to my knees.

It's like a knife that twists inside,
A pain I can't escape,
no matter how hard I've tried.

I want to be happy for you, I truly do,
But it's so hard when all I want is to be with you.

// is she just a distraction?
-nathalie kristine

I wanted this to last

All I ever wanted was a response,
an answer, Or just an explanation.

Anything to stop the constant questioning in my mind.
Why do you take pleasure in knowing I am suffering?

I just want to understand.

// will I ever get my response?
-nathalie kristine

depression

The human heart was not meant to feel this type of ache.
For the most part, I can pretend that I don't feel it.
But then there are moments when my sadness
is so debilitating, my body will begin to shake,
and I can no longer sense reality.

The agony consumes my brain and
I cannot process anything else.
It starts to consumes my bones, I feel like I am rotting.
This constant feeling of ache,
it never seems to stop.
I will force myself to get up, and pretend like I don't feel,
until I can't pretend anymore once again.

// I wasn't meant to feel this type of ache.
-nathalie kristine

I wanted this to last

I don't know why I keep expecting you
to understand how I feel,
You cannot understand something
that you have never felt.

A part of me hopes you never understand,
because this type of ache,
I would never wish on anyone,
not even to the one that caused it.

// Please, try to understand.
-nathalie kristine.

depression

Is it horrible to admit that I still wait for a response?
It's been over a week since I last texted you,
I know you are not going to reply.

Yet every time I hear a notification I hope that it's you.
I'm not going to ever receive a reply am I?

// I already know you won't respond.
-nathalie kristine

I wanted this to last

This depression has made me unrecognizable.
I look in the mirror but I don't see myself.
I see everything I wasn't supposed to be.
I see everything I used to fight not to become.
I don't know who I am.
I only know whoever I am staring at in the mirror,
is not who I wanted to be.

How did I let this overcome me?
What happened to the girl I once was?
I want her back.
You took away everything I knew about myself.

// the loss of love has turned me into someone else.
-nathalie kristine

depression

Sometimes I wonder if you ever read my letters.
I wrote you so many,
maybe you decided they were never worth reading,
maybe I wasted my words,
Maybe you forgot I even wrote you,
Or maybe you did read them
No, that cannot be the case.
If you read them,
how could you continue to say nothing?

If you read my letters,
why didn't you tell me you did?
Surely you wouldn't keep putting me through
the same pain if I ever meant anything to you.

Or maybe you did read them,
and they meant nothing to you.
Maybe you read them and decided you didn't
ever care how you made me feel.

Maybe I will never know the answer.

// would you ever tell me?
-nathalie kristine

I wanted this to last

I don't understand.
why do you keep putting me through the same pain,
I begged you not to, I pleaded with you,
Please just don't make me feel this way again,
it's not impossible what I ask for.

You don't have to love me,
You don't have to choose me,
but you have to be honest with me.

Don't look me in the eyes and tell me you love me,
when you know it's not the truth.

Because I will fall for those sweet puppy eyes,
and believe the lies you say.
That is what puts me in misery.
The ugly truth is better than a sugar-coated lie.

// I can accept the truth, but you won't say it.
-nathalie kristine

depression

I failed.
I failed you.
I failed myself.
I didn't do everything I should have.
I locked you out.
I kept you away from the closest parts of my heart
because I was afraid.

In the end,
the fear of being hurt is what ended up
hurting me the most.
My fear of being abandoned is what
caused me to abandon you.
The fear of suffering is what caused what I suffer now.
I am aware of my faults.
I will no longer let fear be the case anymore.

// I wish I hadn't been so afraid.
-nathalie kristine

I wanted this to last

I wish that you meant as little to me,
as I did to you.

If you had meant nothing to me,
I wouldn't feel this pain.
I would be able to forget how my name sounded
when it came from your lips,
I would easily forget how all our days felt like pure bliss.

I would forget how I made a home in your arms,
and planned a future with your presence.
I wouldn't experience the ache of the past
so deep in my bones.

why does my body feel like
you are all it's ever known.

// I wish you had meant nothing to me.
-nathalie kristine

depression

I can't sleep.
I stay up every night thinking of all the ways
I could have prevented what happened.
Take me back.
Take me back
Oh god please take me back in time.

Take me back to before things
between us were ruined.
I can fix it now.

// I want to go back in time.
-nathalie kristine

I wanted this to last

I attempt to cry you back,
but my tears have stopped and you're still not here.
I have lost count of all the nights I spent crying,
Instead of sleeping.

I call out to you,
no I don't,
it's just an empty room.

a room you are no longer in,
a bed you don't sleep in anymore,
a house you no longer visit.
I attempt to cry you back
But instead,
my tears drown me.

// I thought I would have run of tears by now.
-nathalie kristine

depression

I hate that I find beauty in my sadness.
I do think it is beautiful that I have the capacity
to feel at the extent I do.

It is not something I chose.

My emotional depth was the result of
a child who felt too much anguish.

I know that my sadness won't last forever
but there is a certain comfort it brings.
my ability to grieve until I cannot anymore,
is a part of my identity.

I have never felt just "a little sad"
it is either incomprehensible pain
Or none at all.
So maybe you are lucky,
 you cannot feel the way I do,
but for me,
it is all I have ever known.

// I wish I didn't feel emotion as deeply as I do.
-nathalie kristine

How dramatic of me, how pathetic of me,
to wish to not exist because of something that
never came to be;
because of someone who couldn't care less about me.

But you don't understand how consuming my feelings are.
They consume my thoughts,
they consume my soul,
they consume my lungs,
and take over my ability to speak.
I can't get it to stop no matter how hard I try.

Maybe the only way to stop my suffering is
to let it consume me.
To let myself ache until I cannot anymore,
to cry until there are no more tears left,
to let my legs shake until I can walk again,
and let my thoughts be about you,
until I can finally think of myself.

I may seem pathetic to let myself become
so consumed by how I feel,
but it is the only way
I've ever known how to heal.

// it is only human nature to feel.
-nathalie kristine

depression

I kept wanting to make you a good person,
deep down I know you still are.
But the person you decided to show me was not,
at least not the version of you I got.

It hurts to think that one day
you'll decide to be the person I deserved,
but for someone else.

// I was supposed to have that.
-nathalie kristine

I wanted this to last

My bones are aching with my sadness.
It feels impossible to leave my bed.

My eyes are swollen shut
from all the tears I have shed.
I keep replaying our memories,
over and over in my head.

My hands can no longer write,
from all the paragraphs I sent begging you,
and my heart has sunk so deep
due to what you put me through.

I wonder if you feel this type of agony,
at times I wish you did,
 maybe then you could understand me.

But I know that it's not true,
for you have already replaced me
with somebody new.

// why did you tell me you loved me if you wanted her?
-nathalie kristine

depression

so it was all for nothing.

-nathalie kristine

I wanted this to last

Memories get lonely when you're
the only one who can remember.

my memory is curse;
always reminiscing on the moments
no one else can remember,
as if they never even happened.

What good is being left with remnants of moments
that no one else can recall ?

// my mind Is stuck in a constant state of nostalgia.
-nathalie kristine

depression

It's not fair that I am still thinking of you,
and you probably haven't thought of me at all.

// am I that forgettable?
-nathalie kristine

I wanted this to last

I am running from my despair.
It swallows my heart and bones,
Suddenly I stop running.

My despair has swallowed me entirely,
I am in a state of desolation,
and I can no longer live without being reminded of
how you left me with no explanation.

// why didn't explain anything to me?
-nathalie kristine

depression

Perhaps I am no one,
I cannot escape from my head.
I wish to be alone,
away from everything.

Isolated by peace.

// I want to be alone.
-nathalie kristine

I wanted this to last

Somewhere between then and now
my family went from loving you,
to hating you.

Somewhere between then and now,
my mother went from telling me she hopes
you would be the one I marry,
to telling me I deserved to be treated better.

Somewhere between then and now
It was the hardest thing to do,
I had to watch my whole family
fall out of love with you too.

// in my head I'm happy living in a lie.
-nathalie kristine

depression

I dread the day I forget
the smell of your shampoo.

// could I have stopped you from leaving?
-nathalie kristine

I wanted this to last

I wonder what our last conversation would
have been if we would have known.

I wish I would have hugged you a little tighter,
And memorized your embrace for just a moment longer.
I wish I would have told you that I still love you,
Because I do.
I still love you.

I wonder how different things would be,
if I had only known.

// could I have stopped you from leaving?
-nathalie kristine

depression

It seems that I will always write you letters,
letters that I will never send,

I will fill my notebooks with all the words
I'm too afraid to say, and all the stories I never told.
once the pages have been filled I won't give you those letters,
like I always used to do, Instead I will burn them.

I'll watch the pages filled with all my words
disintegrate into the air.
It's better to burn all of my letters than giving them to you,
knowing they will never be read.

// I wish I never wrote you anything.
-nathalie kristine

I wanted this to last

The loud silence between us,
of what once was a beautiful love

// a love that doesn't exist anymore.
-nathalie kristine

depression

I think I'm meant to be alone,
I'm too much for a lot of people.
Too deep for the shallow,
too emotional for the logical,
too faithful for the sinners,
and too much of a sinner for the faithful.

It becomes lonely,
being too much & too little all at once.

// I wish I wasn't this way.
-nathalie kristine

I wanted this to last

For months I held my tongue for the sake of you,
I kept my suffering quiet,
so you wouldn't know what you put me through.
If you knew how much pain you caused me,
I'm not sure if you'd even be sorry.

You see, only now do I see that you are selfish,
For months you held your tongue, and refused to speak to me,
but only to cause me more suffering.

// did you enjoy having the power to give me pain?
-nathalie kristine

depression

You got the best of me.

You got my purest love
my most tender words,
my most beautiful poems

I will never love another like I have loved you.
You took away the love I had to give.
& now I have nothing left.

// did you enjoy having the power to give me pain?
-nathalie kristine

I wanted this to last

My heart will never be the same,
it carries all the wounds of my love.
I have bandaged them up, and got them to stop bleeding,
only for me to put too much trust in you,
and for you rip those bandages up.

You stabbed my heart to deepen the wounds
that were already there.

// the wounds of love I carry are not scars.
-nathalie kristine

depression

I kept writing to you even after
I had already given you the notebook.
Long after things have ended I still kept writing to you,
just as I had promised to do.

// will you ever read these poems?
 -nathalie kristine

I wanted this to last

Have you ever felt the kind of sadness
that makes your bones feel as if they will decay?

My arms become too heavy,
my legs won't stand on their own,
the depth of the pain is something I have never known.

What is the answer so that I can finally be okay?
my suffering does not rest.

// not even for one day.
-nathalie kristine

depression

Someone just tell me, is it true?
Is it true that you'll never read
all the words I wrote to you?

Who is it that I am writing these poems to?
Deep down I know they are not to you.
Maybe I am writing just to preserve the past,
even though the love we had didn't last.

Maybe I am writing this to someone out there
who understands that sometimes love isn't fair.

A person who can hear the tears
that have stained each poem I wrote,
for I have cried all the pain that is stuck in their throat.

Quite honestly, you will probably never read this,
But at least I know
I am not writing to an empty abyss.

// Maybe my poetry was never meant for you.

nathalie kristine

I wanted this to last

I like to think that in some other life,
we are still together.

// in my head I'm happy living in a lie.
-nathalie kristine

depression

As time continues to pass
I can start to feel other emotions.
I laugh without you
I smile without you
I live without you.

But yet, there is always a deep brooding pit
of sadness in my heart.
I am forever haunted by the ghost
of who you could have been,
of what we could have had,
of how things used to be.
And even though, I can live without you.
I will never smile in the same way I used to.

My eyes will never hold that same kind
of unbroken happiness.
Before they had cried untold amounts of tears;
Before my heart was forced to experience
the very pain I have feared.

the sad reality is that you are not the person
you promised me you'd be,
and my sobs are nothing more than a desperate plea.

// a plea that will never be answered.
-nathalie kristine

I wanted this to last

I haven't let anybody touch me,
hold me,
kiss me,
love me,
not since you left.
So when my heart aches for touch,
my mind can only think of you.

I want the last thing my body to remember
is all the time we spent together.
I don't want to lose all of our memories,
and replace you with someone else,
for they don't deserve to feel
the body you felt.

you may never know,
but I'm still here,
silently loving you.

// I just don't say a word.
-nathalie kristine

depression

You cut the same wound in my heart
 my father had already made.

// only yours cut deeper.
-nathalie kristine

I wanted this to last

I know what it feels like to want to rip
your heart out of your chest,
wishing you could have your last breath.
A type of sadness that makes you long for your own death.

My thoughts are like maggots eating away at my brain,
I simply was not made to feel this much pain.

Why is my brain so misunderstood?

// will there ever be anyone that can understand me?.
   -nathalie kristine

depression

I'll place the blame on anyone else but you,
I refuse to believe that it was all true.

I'd rather blame myself for our downfall,
then choose to hate you for it all.
I could hate myself forever, and assume all the responsibility,
But I do not have the capability,
to blame it all on you.

Not even for any pain you caused,
I understand your pain behind it all,
I'll blame your terrible past, or the circumstances we were in.

It's not your fault we didn't last.

// I refuse to place the blame on you.
  -nathalie kristine

I wanted this to last

acceptance

acceptance

I wanted this to last

I have struggled to accept that you are gone,
because the truth is I don't want to move on.

I choose to believe the lie that you still love me,
rather than accept that we weren't meant to be.
There are days when I feel like my suffering is over,
but then it hits again, and I cannot be sober.
Acceptance has been the most difficult for me,
In my head,
it is still meant to be.

I still hope that our paths cross again even if
we only stay just as friends,
at least then we could both make our amends.

The fact that you left me without saying goodbye,
will always be something that brings tears to my eyes.

I don't know if I will ever fully accept.

// I don't want us to have nothing left.
-nathalie kristine

acceptance

In the end, I can't blame you, can I?
It is not your fault that I chose to love you
more than I loved myself.
It's not your fault that I didn't give up on you even
after you broke all our promises.
It's not your fault I chose to forgive you for things
you would have never forgiven me for.

And as much as I wish I could blame you,
the way I loved you wasn't your fault.

But I refuse to be ashamed of how much I loved you.
I refuse to hate myself for being so committed to loving you,
to feel humiliated for countless times I tried to talk to you.

I am not ashamed of the depth of my love.
I chose to love you at the cost of my sanity.

It is not easy,
but I am choosing to love myself at the same depth,
even at the cost of losing you.

// your love cost me my sanity yet,
I still paid the price.
  -nathalie kristine

I wanted this to last

If you are really over me,
tell me this
If we were both in a crowded room
would your eyes glance at me,
even for only a second?

Or would you not even notice I was there?

// do you search for me in croweded rooms?
-nathalie kristine

acceptance

I want my pain to end, when will this be over?
it's been 9 months now,
I just want some closure.
I want to end our chapter, not just bookmark the page;
convincing myself whats left of us,
I can save.

I have not stopped loving you, even from afar.
but now, my heart has been covered in scars.
I already know, in order to heal my heart,
I have to let you go.
But you came back, and finally gave me an explanation,
an answer to all my desperation.

you told me for months you had been
planning to commit suicide.
you wanted to make me hate you,
In hopes that it would hurt me less,
But I cannot bring myself to hate you,
even after everything you put me through,
It is still so easy for me to forgive you.
That is because I understand you.

I want to take away all your pain,
but my own suffering still remains.
the way you have treated me has torn me apart.
But it still hurts me,
seeing you in pain.

// please don't give up.
 -nathalie kristine

As much as I want to hate you for everything you did,
there is an angel on my shoulder,
and she whispers in my ear,

"he is only a hurt soul…
just like you my dear."

// I can't hate you.
-nathalie kristine

acceptance

our relationship has been long over,
and we have not been sober.
so please,
do not pull me any closer.

all I wanted was some closure.

// I can't hate you.
-nathalie kristine

I wanted this to last

Our love was once in a lifetime,
I will never love anyone the way I loved you.
Maybe that is for the best.

I will never again love someone
to the point of self-destruction,
Even though,
it was beautiful to have the capability
to destroy myself for you.

// I will never love another as deeply as I loved you.
   -nathalie kristine

acceptance

I wasn't ever ready to say goodbye to you,
I still have not said it.

I'm sorry that we both let things end like this.

// I can't help feeling like it wasn't supposed too.
-nathalie kristine

I wanted this to last

Grieving isn't linear I've learned,
Some days I wake up and you're not on my mind,
not in my prayers or conversations,
and the pain of loss I no longer find.

But then there are those other days,
when thoughts of you take over my heart,
consuming me, I feel the ache,
I clutch my heart to ease the pain.

I wish I could break free,
From all this pain that's consuming me,
I don't know how much more I can take,
but I'll keep moving through the ache.

// sometimes my grief takes me back in time.
  -nathalie kristine

acceptance

I long for God.

To be without God,
 is to be a prisoner of an evil world.

Despite it all,
I pray I will meet you again.

Perhaps in heaven
Or
Perhaps not.

// I ask God to let our paths cross again
  -nathalie kristine

I wanted this to last

I wouldn't say that we are strangers now,
I still know how many freckles you
have on both your cheeks,
and all the recipes that you used to cook me.
I still know what you like to wear to bed,
and about your struggles with your fathers death.

I still know all the little things about you.
I wonder if you still remember mine too.

I don't know what to call us,
but you are not a stranger.

Whatever we are now,
I still remember the way we used to be.

// parts of you always linger.
  -nathalie kristine

acceptance

All humans seek understanding.
Revenge is sought to hurt people
the same way they hurt you.
Why?
Because at least then,
they would understand the agony you felt.
at least then,
you wouldn't be alone in your suffering.

If only there was a way to make those who hurt you
understand the pain without going through it themselves.

If only there were more
understanding in the hearts of others.

// I don't want revenge,
I want to be understood.
-nathalie kristine

I wanted this to last

For months I have been missing you,
but today something changed.

Something feels different.

I saw a picture of you with another girl,
It didn't hurt me like I thought it used too.
I felt a sad sense of peace.
I felt acceptance.
Maybe it's okay that you are no longer mine,
I can finally move on knowing you have moved on too.
That doesn't mean I will forget you,
you are a permanent part of my past.

You were my first love,
just not my last.

// I maybe our love wasn't meant to last.
  -nathalie kristine

acceptance

I never thought I would feel grateful for
the pain you put me through,
But I do.

At first it changed me in the worst way possible,
I became the very person I swore I'd never be.
I couldn't handle the pain I felt,
I became someone so unrecognizable.
You destroyed me,
but I rebuilt myself.

I got myself up every morning,
I made sure I ate,
I read myself books,
I tucked myself in,
I let myself feel.

I took the pain you left me with,
and made it into something beautiful.
I could have never done the things I have
without all my suffering.

Thank you for all that you put me through.
I am no longer bitter.
I am better.

// I have so much more strength.
-nathalie kristine

I wanted this to last

I've started to adjust to your absence.
You're no longer my first thought in the morning,
or my last thought at night.
But still whenever something good, or bad happens to me,
I think of you.
My mind goes back to the days when we'd tell
each other everything and for a moment,
I almost reach for my phone to call you.

Then I remember,
You are not the boy that lives in my memory
You are someone else now.

/ I miss the boy that only exists in my memory.
  -nathalie kristine

acceptance

It's funny looking back on the past
 without the rose-colored glasses,
I see now all the ways you continuously
took advantage of me.

I must admit our relationship was almost perfect.
We were almost perfect,
we almost made it too.
But once we were over, you became someone else,
a person I never knew.
Someone who didn't care for my existence.

Maybe you are not a bad person,
but the person you chose to be to me was bad.
You chose to lead me to your bed,
and whisper sweet lies in my head.
Just so you could leave without saying goodbye.

I think you enjoyed seeing me in pain,
And I let it happen just so that I could be
in your presence once again.

// no one could ever love you the way I do.
-nathalie kristine

I wanted this to last

You have changed me.
In ways I would have
never been able to change myself.
It's funny to think you helped create
the best version of me,
but also the worst.

// you don't know how much you affected me.
-nathalie kristine

acceptance

I am finally becoming the girl I was always meant to be.

The one who lives in sun's embrace,
 and never let's the smile fade from her face.
It was my weakness that has me so strong.
The one that lets happiness flow from her insides,
The one that dances under the moon,
The girl that I have always been,
underneath all my suffering.

// I was never the person my pain made me.
-nathalie kristine

I wanted this to last

I now understand what it is like to miss someone,
you do not want back in your life.
today you are like a stranger I pass on the street,
someone that I don't want to meet.

Yet when I sit alone in a restaurant chair,
I stare at the empty space and I picture you there.

I think I will always reminisce on what we could have been,
but that is something that will never happen.

We were only so close.
you will always be my almost.

// Sometimes I talk aloud and pretend as if you were still here.
  -nathalie kristine

acceptance

I have made peace with your silence,
Maybe I'll never get my answer.

Maybe you'll read my poems and finally understand,
or maybe you won't.
Maybe we'll get a chance to start over.
or maybe we don't.
Maybe our paths will cross again,
or maybe we'll go in opposite directions.

But I finally made peace in not knowing,
and I'll be ok if we never spoke again.

// you are becoming a distant memory.
-nathalie kristine

I wanted this to last

Your silence was my explanation,
It was not because I wasn't worthy of an answer,
It was because you wanted to run away,
 from your own emotions,
from all of your pain.

You'd rather pretend I never existed,
than admit your own faults.

// I began to listen to the silence.
-nathalie kristine

acceptance

I wanted this to last

I will admit it hurt to see you with her at first.
It doesn't hurt anymore.
It is quite the opposite,
if you can find another one to love.

I think that maybe one day I will too.

// I wish you luck with your someone new.
-nathalie kristine

acceptance

When I met you my heart was in pieces,
and you made my broken heart whole.
Only to break it in ways it had never been broken before.
I crawled back begging you to fix again once more;
only you didn't this time,
and you watched as I suffered.

I have now mended my own wounds,
and I will never need another person to pick up my pieces.
I learned healing is my responsibility, never will I place
the pieces of my wounded heart
into the hands of the one who broke it.

// I have healed my own heart.
-nathalie kristine

I wanted this to last

Looking back,
everything that happened wasn't for the best,
but I have finally taken the knife out of my chest.

I have learned that nothing in this life will last,
and that time will pass by much too fast.
I will cherish every memory I make,
and never get rid of the pictures I take.

No matter how much we wanted this to last,
we are now only a part of each others past.

// at least we had that short time together.
  -nathalie kristine

acceptance

Life went on,
I moved houses, and so did you.

I got a new job,
and so did too.

I changed my hair, got new clothes,
and you did too.

I got new friends, met new people
that you'll never know about,
and so did too.

I experienced new things,
made new memories, ones without you in them,
and you did too.
It was never the same,
and it never will be again.

But life continues to go on,
and slowly we forget what we once knew.

// but sometimes I'm still reminded of you.
-nathalie kristine

I wanted this to last

In the end, I am thankful for you
I know we both hurt each other in ways
 the other will never understand,

But we both loved each other in ways
no one else could ever comprehend.

Thank you for loving me
Thank you for hurting me too,
without the pain of losing love,
I would have never known I had it.

 I guess there were good things that came from your absence.

// I will never forget the way we loved each other...
-nathalie kristine

acceptance

There was a time when I knew all your dreams and
aspirations, we had a life plan that we used to share.
But now, things have changed,
and life has proved it's unfair.
You've moved on,
and I was left with a deep pain to repair.

So now I stand all alone,
and I've made different plans of my own.
I don't need to know about your life anymore,
just go on, find what you've been looking for.

I'll let go of the past and set myself free,
and I'll find the life path that was meant for me.

// I hope you get everything you want,
and I hope I never hear a thing about it.
-nathalie kristine

I wanted this to last

Maybe it did take losing the person I loved most,
 to be able to actually love myself.

Maybe life knew that the only way I'd ever understand
who I am was to rip away the person
I placed my false identity in.

// you became a part of me.
-nathalie kristine

acceptance

I deserve to be written about in the ways I write about you.
I deserve to be taken care of,
in the same ways I used to take care of you.
I deserve to be understood,
in the same way I understand.

I deserve someone willing to wait for my body,
in the same way I was so willing to save it for you

I deserve someone who will read my poetry,
 and marvel at my mind,
I deserve to be loved in the ways I love.

I deserved an answer,
I deserved an explanation,
or at the very least I deserved a goodbye.

You have taught me that I deserve far more than
you could have ever given me,
but not in a bitter way.

it is not your fault,
you had no idea how to love a girl
who loved too much.

// I deserve better.
-nathalie kristine

I wanted this to last

even though we didn't last,
you will always be the best part of my past.

// and my favorite memory.
-nathalie kristine

acceptance

I don't think things happened for the best
but
I decided to the make the best out
of the things that happened.

// I'm sorry.
-nathalie kristine

I wanted this to last

If one day your children stumble across
the notebook filled with letters,
or our unfinished scrapbook,
and they ask you who I was,
Tell them everything.

Tell them about our love story and the tragic ending,
teach them about loss, and the hope that comes after.
Let the lessons we learned from each other,
help prevent our children of the pain we suffered.

I promise to tell my children about you,
I'll tell them all the stories about everywhere we went,
our first kiss,
about the summer we had spent,
and most importantly the lessons I have learned from you.

// I will always remember what you taught me.
-nathalie kristine

acceptance

As our story ends,
I want you to know that I forgive you.
I don't hate you for what you put me through,
I am grateful for it now.

As much as I hate to admit it,
The tears that came from all my pain,
are what watered the seeds of change.

// now I am able to grow
-nathalie kristine

I wanted this to last

In your arms I once thought I had found my forever,
I guess my forever only lasted two years.

Can I make one last request?
No matter how much time passes,
no matter how many other people we meet,
how many other people we love,
promise me that you won't forget me,
and all the things we did?

Promise me that you won't throw away my letters,
or delete all our pictures?

Promise that you will let our love be
a beautiful thing of the past,
something to be remembered,
and not to be erased.

Promise me that one day,
when your children ask for bedtime stories,
you'll still tell them about ours
even though,
we never got our happy ending.

// I'll still tell my kids about you.
-nathalie kristine

acceptance

If I never get to talk to you again,
I want you to know that I'm proud of you.

You are such an incredible soul, you've come so far.
I'm so grateful that I got to be a part of your life.
I want you to know that I always loved you,
and even now I still do.
I don't want to move on but I know I have too.

I'll never love anybody the same way I loved you,
know that you will always be special to me.

// I will never write about anyone the way I wrote about you.
-nathalie kristine

I wanted this to last

I never thought I'd be able to move on,
but I did.

Your name no longer hurts my lips when I speak of you.
My hands no longer search for yours when they feel cold.
My eyes no longer crave to see the corners of your smile.
My ears no longer want to hear you whisper my name.
My heart is no longer yours,
my heart is my own now.

// I don't belong to you like I used too.
-nathalie kristine

acceptance

I will always carry remnants of you with me.

// your flowers are still hung up on my walls.
-nathalie kristine

I wanted this to last

I no longer fear acceptance.
months have passed and we haven't spoke,
and the thought of you doesn't fill my mind
as much as it used to.

I don't remember what your arms used feel like
when they'd wrap around me, or what your smile
looked like every time you saw me.
I am starting to forget the sound of your voice,
and I can hardly remember the smell of your cologne.

I don't live in the same house that I used to,
My clothes are all new,
ones you've never seen me wear.
My hair is no longer the natural brunette you said
I looked prettiest in.

We are both different people now.

I am no longer haunted by the empty promises you gave me,
I have found my answers in your silence,
The pain you caused me has changed me,
for the better.

Maybe forgetting you isn't so bad.

// but there are certain memories that will always stay.
-nathalie kristine

acceptance

To truly be the one that got away,
you have to be the one that doesn't stay.

The one that will not put up with their selfish acts,
a woman who keeps herself intact.
The one that won't go crawling back,
the woman who chooses to face the facts.

Not every man you love will stay,
but I promise you it is meant to be that way.

So please,
allow yourself to hurt.
But darling,
don't forget your worth.

// you deserve to be loved the way you love.
-nathalie kristine

I wanted this to last

I can finally say I am over you.
Truly.

Even if you decided to give me the call
that I've been waiting for,
I wouldn't answer.
Even if you decided to send a response
to the paragraphs I texted months ago,
I wouldn't reply.

But just know if they ever invent time machines,
I would spend every last penny to go back
and save what we once had.

// I am moving forward,
but I will always look for a way back.
-nathalie kristine

acceptance

Goodbye, I release you now,
even though it hurts my heart to allow,
I promise I will never forget you.
our love has reached an end,
and it's time we both made our amends.

The memories we shared will always remain,
But dwelling on what's lost will only bring more pain.
I'll treasure the moments we had so close,
you will always be my almost.

Though it's hard to move on and start anew,
I'll find the strength to see it through.
I'll cherish the lessons you taught me well,
we'll both move forward,
with a heartbreaking story to tell.

// I will cherish you forever.
-nathalie kristine

I wanted this to last

I promise to meet you in another life,
but this time we will do it right.

me + you

acceptance

Made in the USA
Las Vegas, NV
17 January 2024